Dedicated to the late, great Dr David Allen, Senior Lecturer and College Dean of Mattersey Hall Bible College from 1982-2005 who inspired me to learn from the past, to live in the present and to look forward to the future.

INTRODUCTION

*'These things happened to them as examples and were
written down as warnings for us....' (1 Cor. 10:11)*

What's the point of 'history?'[1] As a teacher of Early Church this
is a question I have often been asked by students over the years.
Some would quote the Apostle Paul's: 'Forgetting what is **behind**
and straining towards what is **ahead**, I press on....' (Phil. 3:13-14a).
We have George Bernard Shaw's often quoted dictum: 'Hegel was
right when he said that we learn from history that man can never
learn from history' together with Henry Ford's: 'History is bunk!'
Many, no doubt in our 'now' generation, would agree with these
sentiments and ask: 'Why on earth study figures from the past?
Why not confine our reading to the present? Why read about
people with whom we might not agree?'

In my view, firstly, we need a knowledge of the past to **understand**
the present. People without a grasp of history are like people
without a memory. Many of our current beliefs and practices in
both the Church and society are properly grasped only when we
see how they have emerged and developed. Some knowledge of
history will help us to understand both ourselves and those with
whom we might disagree. Secondly, we need knowledge of the
past to **escape** the present. History does have a habit of repeat-
ing itself and if the lessons of the past are not learnt the same
mistakes will often happen again. The same Apostle Paul, who
encouraged the believers at Philippi to 'forget what is behind', also
exhorted the Corinthian believers to take note that the experi-
ences of the Children of Israel in the wilderness *happened to them
as examples and were written down as warnings*' to future gener-

ations (1 Cor. 10:11).

How, then, should we view the past? According to Tony Lane, there are two main ways to approach history. Some treat it as a *mirror* in which they admire their own reflections – they study the characters and events with which they are familiar and perhaps comfortable with. However, the best approach to history is to treat is as a *window*. A window is there to look outside, to see something new and to be challenged to change and learn.[2]

CHAPTER 1 THE POWER OF PENTECOST

'But you will receive power when the Holy
Spirit comes on you....' (Acts 1:8)

In my view, one of the greatest miracles of the Early Church era is how the Church of Jesus Christ was started, grew, spread and triumphed against all the odds and despite tremendous pressure. As the Emmaus Road encounter teaches us in Luke 24:13-35, at least some of the disciples, after the crucifixion of Jesus, had become a group of disillusioned and scattered 'sheep' who had lost their Shepherd. However, after receiving a clear mandate from the Risen Christ in Acts 1:8 and having been filled with the promised Holy Spirit on the Day of Pentecost, these same disciples were transformed into people of power who both preached with signs following and died a martyr's death for the message they believed and proclaimed.[3] Luke tells us in the sequel to his Gospel, that 3000 were converted after one single sermon in Acts 2. By Acts 5, another 2000 were added and the first disciples of Christ had '*filled Jerusalem with their teaching*' (v28). By Acts 17 they had 'turned the world upside down' (v6) and historians tell us that by 112 AD, in a certain Roman province, every village had been Christianised. By 500 AD, the Roman Empire was predominantly 'Christian' in name if not always in nature.

There are various factors that caused the Early Church to be established and expand so quickly - these include:

1) *Signs and wonders*
It would be safe to say that outreach in the Book of Acts

was preaching, persuasion, presence but also power – with almost every act of public evangelism being backed up with a display of the supernatural. For example, the Day of Pentecost in Acts 2, Peter & John at the gate called 'Beautiful' in Acts 3, Philip the Evangelist in Samaria in Acts 8 to name but a few. Signs and wonders, followed by a clear presentation of the Good News saw many added to the Church - certainly a fulfilment of the words of Christ, that certain 'signs' will accompany clear Gospel-preaching (Mk. 16:15-18).

2) The Roman rule

At the time of Christ and the establishment of his Church, the Romans were in power. Their rule brought the *Pax Romana*, or Roman Peace, and the provinces within the Roman Empire enjoyed almost unbroken peace for much of the time. Roads were cleared of robbers, the seas of pirates, all major roads did lead to Rome, the roads and bridges were well built, there was a common currency and people could travel without the need for documentation. Irenaeus, in the 2nd century AD, sums these times up well:

> *'The world has peace, thanks to the Romans. Even Christians can walk without fear on the roads and travel whithersoever they please.'[4]*

Such ease of travel around the empire, together with the fact that Roman citizens, such as the Apostle Paul, were allowed special privileges including protection and a fair trial, aided the Gospel of Christ in its rapid spread from Jerusalem to the ends of the earth in a relatively short space of time.

3) The Greek language

Though the Romans were the political rulers of the then known world, it was the Greek language and thoughts the dominated its culture. The motto of the late, great Alexander-the Great was *'one language and one world'* and through both himself and his successors a commitment to *Hellenisation*, or the enforcing and fostering of Greek language, thought, philosophy and architecture was established and became long lasting across many parts of the world. Within a short space of time, Greek became the language of both rulers and slaves, the soldiers and the merchants, the rich and poor. Letters, poetry and business communications were all written in Greek and when the Romans came to power, they found in the Greek language an ideal way to communicate with their captured territories as well as in a common language to bring unity to the Roman Empire. However, for the Early Church, Greek became a matchless vehicle for spreading the Christian message. Because the language was so widely used, the apostles could preach in Greek almost anywhere in the Empire without the need for interpreters. The widespread use of the language, certainly by the 1st century, also explains why all of the New Testament, written mostly by Jews, was first written in Greek. When the gospel came, there was a worldwide language in which it could be communicated, again causing its rapid spread.

4) *The believers gossiping the Gospel*

Although the Apostle Paul stated his ambition was to *'preach Christ where he is not known...'* (Rom. 15:20), the task of world evangelisation in the 1st century was certainly not Paul's alone. According to Early Church historian, Eusebius, the first disciples were:

> *'Dispersed over the whole world, with Parthia allotted to Thomas, Ethiopia to Matthew, India to Bartholomew, Scythia to Andrew, Asia to John and Asia Minor to Peter....'*[5]

However, the work of witnessing was not limited to the first apostles either, it was clearly a work of the whole Church, where the average believer *'felt themselves to be more or less in a state of mission.'*[6] Origen, in the 3rd century, observes:

'Christians leave no stone unturned to spread the faith in all parts of the world. Some, in fact, have done the work of going round not only in cities but even villages and country cottages to make others also pious towards God.'[7]

This sense of ownership of the responsibility to share the Good News by all believers is borne out by Luke when he states that:

'Those who had been scattered preached the word wherever they went' (Acts 8:4).

5) The Christian reaction to persecution

As will be seen in the next chapter, persecution for the Early Church from the 1st to 4th centuries was a clear and present danger with many negatives including internal division, loss of life, confiscation of property and martyr-worship. However, there was clearly a positive dimension to persecution as seen in Tertullian's often-quoted warning to the Emperor at the time:

'Your cruelty against us does not profit you. Instead it tempts people to our sect. As often as you mow us down, the more we grow in number. The blood of the Christian is the seed of the Church. For who when seeing [our faith] is not excited to enquire what lies behind it? Who, having enquired, does not embrace it?'[8]

The suffering and death of Christians had a definite magnetic appeal to the unbeliever. In addition, during such persecution the Christians were encouraged to remain loyal to the authorities and willing to carry out the commands of Rome, as much as it allowed, despite the miscarriage of justice done to them. The 'Epistle to Diognetus' from the 2nd or 3rd century states the response of the persecuted to their persecutors:

'They love those that hated them'

Tertullian, again, states that:

> *'Christians call upon God for the safety of the Emperor. They pray for their enemies and entreat blessings for their persecutors.'[9]*

It would be no exaggeration to say that Christians, on the whole, were willing to die for their faith. Ignatius of Antioch, when writing to the Romans at the beginning of the 2nd century, exclaimed:

> *'I die for Christ of my own choice. Let me be given to the wild beasts.....'[10]*

There is a stirring account of Bishop Polycarp of Smyrna's martyrdom which survives in *The Letter to the Smyrneans on the Martyrdom of Polycarp*. The Roman governor tried to persuade the aged bishop to deny Christ in order to gain his freedom, but he replied:

> *'Eighty and six years I have served Him and he has done me no wrong. How can I then blaspheme my King who saved me?'*

Reasons for an individual's willingness to die for Christ can only be guessed at. Perhaps, martyrdom was seen as the ultimate mark of discipleship according to Jesus' own words in Mark 8:34 or their Master's warning of expected suffering in John 15:20 was taken most seriously. However, what we can be certain of is this - the Church's attitude of forgiveness and blessing towards its enemies, in line with the command of Jesus in Matt. 5:44, together with its general willingness to suffer and die for the cause of Christ, resulted in an unbelieving world sitting up and taking notice and for some to go a step further and join the Christian Faith themselves.

Persecution for the Early Church continued for some 280 years after the Day of Pentecost. However, as will be seen, this was not the only problem that faced the Church throughout this time.

CHAPTER 2   PROBLEMS FROM WITHOUT AND PROBLEMS FROM WITHIN

'In this world you will have trouble....' (John 16:33)

It is evident from both the exposition of Scripture and human experience, that when God's people obey Him and move forward into His plan and purpose, opposition is not far away. This was certainly Paul's experience – for example, in Ephesus, he experienced both a door of opportunity and a door of opposition (1 Cor. 16:8-9) and from Acts 19, he had experienced both a riot and a revival in the same city. There is the well-known example of Nehemiah - as he gained success in the building of the walls and gates of Jerusalem, opposition soon arose in the form of Sanballat, Tobiah and Geshem, (Nehemiah 2:19ff). For the Early Church it was no different. Before 64 AD, although experiencing some persecution from the Jews, its existence was generally tolerated by the Roman Empire - but soon all of that changed under the rule of Emperor Nero. In 64 AD, there was a huge fire that destroyed a large part of Rome and, as a scapegoat was needing to be found, the Christians were blamed. Almost overnight Christianity went from being a legal religion to a *religio illicita* and ten main periods of persecution followed until the reign of Constantine in the early 4th century. In addition to being easy targets of blame for the fire, the Christians were persecuted for such reasons as:

1) *Their exclusiveness*
   Christians were generally considered by the common people and authorities as 'separatists' and in many ways anti-social.

Their moral standards were different from that of the pagan and they were thus hated because of their puritanical way of life.

2) They were viewed as 'atheists'

Due to the fact that Christians did not offer sacrifices and worship to the many gods of Rome, which was a practice expected for Roman subjects except Jews, they were viewed as 'atheists'.[11] Because of this, when a natural disaster occurred or a battle was lost, the Christians were blamed as the Roman authorities believed that pagan gods were offended

3) The believers' meetings

The Early Church meeting caused rumours amongst society. The Agape Love Feast, or Communion Service, was viewed as an orgy, cannibalism was suspected when it was heard that 'flesh' was eaten and 'blood' drank and the practice of a 'holy kiss' was misunderstood!

4) The Christian attitude to slavery

To the pagan, a slave during biblical times was generally viewed as a piece of property that was often subject to abuse and misuse and someone without rights or liberty. However, Christian teaching in the Scriptures encouraged the fair treatment of slaves (e.g. Col. 4:1) and a plain reading of Paul's Letter to Philemon could well indicate the viewing of a Christian slave as a 'brother' in Christ.

5) Disloyalty to Rome

Arguably the main reason for persecution was due to the fact that the Roman authorities did not believe that Christians were loyal to the State, who demanded complete submission as a prerequisite for peace. Although the Christians were in fact loyal subjects as commanded by Paul (see Rom. 13:1ff) and in many ways useful to society, especially during times of famine and plague, their allegiance was firstly to Christ and not to Caesar. Such 'stubbornness' led to trials for treason and martyrdom for many who refused to participate in pagan worship ceremonies.

Although it would be safe to say that the Church experienced periods of peace throughout the 250 years of persecution, it was generally a brutal and cruel time where multitudes perished for their faith and where, according to Tacitus, the Christian was regarded as 'an enemy of the human race.'[12]

However, during the Early Church era, in addition to persecution – an attack from without, there was the very real threat and reality of heresy – an attack from within. From the pages of the New Testament and the writings of Peter, Paul and John, false teaching and 'another gospel' (Gal. 1:8) in the various assemblies was both present and promised and during the course of time, and on many occasions, the Church needed to defend and contend for the Faith as well as clearly defining what it did believe. The Church was able to defend itself in two main ways – through the ministry of Apologists[13] such as Tertullian, Justin Martyr, Origen and Irenaeus who, on a mainly intellectual and philosophical level, defended the Truth – and also through the gathering of councils and the production of creeds. Regarding the latter, when a controversy arose – usually concerning the Trinity, Person of Christ or the Holy Spirit – a council of bishops and priests would gather from either a particular locality or from further afield to discuss and debate the particular issue at great length with various views presented. After a majority or unanimous agreement was reached a creed,[14] or statement of belief, was produced which gave clarity to the wider Church on a point of doctrine that needed both protecting and promoting.

Popular heresies during the first four centuries that were tackled head-on by the Church include Arianism and its denial of the true divinity of Christ, Apollinarism and its belief that Jesus could not have had a human mind and Macedonianism and its un-acceptance of the divinity of the Holy Spirit.

Although the problem of heresy continued, and still continues to this day, the problem of persecution on this epic scale did end for the Early Church due to the efforts of one Flavius Valerius Aurelius Constantinius Augustus – or Constantine the Great.

CHAPTER 3   CONSTANTINE – A HELP OR A HINDRANCE?

'..choose you this day whom you will serve.' (Josh. 24:15)

The last main periods of State persecution for the Church occurred under Emperors Diocletian (284-305) and Galerius (305-311). The former, as a last ditched effort to eradicate Christianity once and for all, issued an edict in 303 AD which declared that all church buildings be demolished, Scripture burnt, Church leaders removed and members enslaved if sacrifices were not made to the idols of Rome. Galerius, similarly, continued to suppress the Church though tradition tells us that as he lay dying he issued an edict of toleration in order to gain the favour and prayers of the Christians.

In 312 AD a momentous event took place that became a major turning point not only for the Church but also affected the history of European civilisation. After the demise of Emperor Galerius in 311, there was a mad scramble for power within the Roman Empire. Constantine and Maxentius, rulers in the West, met for battle at Milvian Bridge to contest for the title of Western Emperor and the events that occurred, just prior to battle, are worth re-counting, although the details are sometimes disputed. According to the historian Eusebius, in his biography *The Life of Constantine* written some years after the event, Constantine prayed first for the help of his father's favourite deity, the *Sol Invictus* or the 'Unconquered Sun'. Shortly after, in late afternoon, a cross appeared in the sky above the sun together with the words *In hoc signo vinces* – 'By this sign you shall conquer.' From this came the famous standard of Constantine, a spearhead forming the cross with the *Chi Rho*, the initial Greek letters of the name Christ, enclosed in a circle. From that time on Constantine considered himself to be a Christian. Although doubts have been expressed about the depth and sincerity of his 'faith', the fact remains that shortly after the events at Milvian Bridge, Constantine and Licinius, ruler of the East and who were now left to share the Empire between them, met at Milan in 313 AD. It would appear that on this occasion an edict or policy of toleration was made and the ban on Christianity, in place since the days of Nero in the 1st century, was lifted. Attitudes towards the Church began to change – Christians were free to worship, their confiscated property restored, ministers and priests were exempt from taxation, funds were made available for churches to be built, Sunday became a holiday for all and clergy adopted a form of dress as their distinctive attire. In addition, other 'fruits of repentance' were displayed with the passing of laws that forbade 'black magic' and the private consulting of mediums,[15] the fairer treatment of slaves, criminals, children and even animals and with Christians being encouraged to take office as magistrates in the community.

In 323 AD, the partnership of Constantine and Licinius turned to rivalry and at the Battle of Chrysopolis, Lincinus was utterly defeated. Constantine decided to rule alone with an advisory council at arms' length and with this new form of government and new 'religion' a new capital for the Empire was needing to be found. Eventually, Byzantium, later known as Constantinople after the Emperor's death in 337 AD and Istanbul in 1930, was decided upon – its seven hills commanded the approaches to both Europe and Asia and its narrow straits joined the East and the West, conducive to effective communication. As sole ruler, Constantine's primary task was to restore and preserve the unity of his vast empire. There were two main considerations – religion, as almost one-tenth of the total population at this time professed to be Christian and organisation, i.e. keeping together the East and the West. With regards to religion, as his reign progressed Constantine supported the Christians increasingly and perhaps saw within his newfound faith, the cement that would bind together the entire Roman Empire.

'Almost overnight it was the done thing to be a Christian'.[16] Ministers or priests received honour and prestige and together with exemption from tax the temptation was, no doubt, to enter 'the ministry' for wrong reasons. Christianity in the Empire at the beginning of Constantine's reign was approximately 10% of the total population whereas post-Constantine this rose dramatically to 50%. Although it would be incorrect to say these were all cosmetic conversions, history does show that the Church after Constantine did lose its way. Pagan temples began to be transformed into Christian shrines, pagan festivals were Christianised and a new trend of pilgrimage to 'holy places' was set after the Emperor's mother had a church built over the place in Bethlehem where the Christ-child was supposedly born. Later, there was the prominence of the local priest as the 'go-between' man and God, the rise of the Pope, the introduction of Latin, traditions replacing the Bible as the rule of faith and the Church claiming final authority in all areas of life from the cradle to the casket.

Sadly, the Church that had begun in the power of the Spirit on the Day of Pentecost became pampered and to many grew increasingly spiritually ineffective. This resulted in the growth of a new movement amongst the Church laity called 'monasticism'[17] which saw many live apart from the world, whether as solitaries, in communities of like-minded individuals or a combination of both. Such a way of life gave the perceived opportunity to not only save oneself from being tarnished from a decaying Church but also to allow the time and freedom from responsibilities to contemplate, study and pray. Although such ascetic living did cause some weird and wonderful goings on with the examples of the 'pillar saints', those that ate nothing but grass and those that sought to self-harm in order to outdo others in the pursuit of 'holiness', generally those who adopted the monastic life did seek to reach out to their world in a spiritual and social sense with Christ being preached and the monastery becoming a place of refuge, care and learning.

As regards Constantine's personal conviction, the most diverse views have been, and still are, held. Was he a genuine Christian who whole-heartedly accepted the faith and teaching of the Church and Scripture? Was he really a syncretist whose desire was to mesh together various belief systems in order to establish a universal religion that would keep the majority happy? Was he an astute politician and statesman who believed he could find in Christianity the social and moral force that would bring unity to his empire? The debate on Constantine's personal motivation will go on but one thing is sure, after 313 AD the Church began to change and many would say decay. As time progressed the ease with which Christianity could be practiced brought many unworthy elements into the Church and helped lower its standard. Although it is true that Constantine's reign inaugurated a great physical move forward in Christianity, a movement in which he himself assisted not only by his legislation but also by his grand building projects, spiritually speaking it was arguably a different matter. Constantine led the Church to becoming the official State religion. Gone now was the 'blood of the martyrs' and the persecuted and at times the Church became the persecutor. The wars in the Empire developed into holy wars and the Church became wealthy and powerful. Shortly after Constantine, the 'Dark Age' for the Church began.

CHAPTER 4   BRIGHT LIGHTS IN A DARK AGE

'You are the light of the world. A town built on a hill cannot be hidden.' (Matt. 5:14)

The 'Dark Ages' is a term sometimes applied to the period of the Middle Ages after the fall of Rome in the 5th century AD. Some would say the term applies to an intellectual darkness characteristic of the times, others would say it refers to the 'darkness' of culture and art which ended with the 'light' of the Renaissance, or rebirth, from the 14th century onwards. Christian historians would see the concepts of 'dark' and 'light' in more sacred terms.

With the latter in mind, spiritual highlights, or some may say 'lowlights,' of the Dark Ages include:

1) **The rise of the Pope**

   After the establishment of the Church in the 1st century as time progressed the Bishop of Rome, or the Pope,[18] gained in importance. There were various reasons for this – Rome was, initially, the capital of the Roman Empire and the congregation in Rome soon numbered many thousands by the year 250 AD. For better or for worse, bishops or leaders of large congregations in important centres of trade, government and culture tended to be regarded as more important than other bishops. From as early as the end of the 1st century, the Bishop of Rome was looked to for leadership – e.g. Bishop Clement 1, when writing to the Corinthian Church and intervening in a dispute, apologises for not having taken action earlier. In the late 2nd century the Christians of Southern Gaul, or modern-day France, pleaded to Rome for toleration of the Montanists[19] and Irenaeus stated that 'with the Church of Rome, because of its superior origin, all the churches must agree....'[20] In 254 AD a serious dispute regarding baptism broke out between Stephen, the Bishop of Rome, and Cyprian, the Bishop of Carthage. Stephen sought to settle the dispute by stating that as he 'sat in Peter's chair, he alone should rule on important matters such as the sacraments.'[21]

When Constantine came to the throne his patronage to the Church included the giving of one of the imperial palaces, the Lateran, to the Pope at the time in addition to extensive lands in central Italy. From this time onwards, the Bishop of Rome living in a palace became both symbolic and prophetic as the Pope became increasingly regarded as Head of Church in the same way that the Emperor was acknowledged as the political ruler. Because many of the emperors after Constantine professed to be 'Christian' both the Pope and Emperor ruled side by side as close allies. Instead of being a humble shepherd, as were the early ministers who served the flock of God in Early Church times (cf. 1 Peter 5:2-3), the Pope is now able to hold his own with kings and even beat them at the diplomatic game. In later medieval times, popes played powerful roles in Europe, often contending with monarchs for control over the wide-ranging affairs of Church and State, crowning emperors and regulating disputes among secular rulers.

2) The fall of the Roman Empire

A major event during the early 'Dark Ages' was the fall of the Western Roman Empire. The Empire had lasted over 500 years at its most powerful its territories included lands in West Europe, the lands around the Mediterranean, Britain, Asia Minor and North Africa. The decline of the Empire is the subject of debate and study, was due to many causes and over several hundred years. Historians are generally agreed that Rome, itself, was sacked in 410 AD, the first time in 800 years that the city had fallen to a foreign enemy and the Western Roman Empire fell some years later on September 4th 476 AD when Romulus Augustus was deposed by Odovacar, a Germanic chieftain. The main causes of the fall included the constant wars with its heavy military spending, the cost of gladiatorial games, the decline of ethics and morals, natural disasters and the on-going Barbarian invasions.

3) Changes in the Church

The 'Dark Ages' saw a radical change in Church doctrine and practice and a pulling away from New Testament teaching. For example, infant sprinkling replaced the baptism of believers by full immersion and the primitive Breaking of Bread service became an elaborate ritual where the emblems ceased to be merely symbolic but literally changed into the very body and blood of Christ after consecration by the priest. Other far-fetched doctrines soon emerged including the belief in an intermediate place called Purgatory, prayers offered for the dead and to the saints, the adoration of Mary as *Theotokos*, or the 'Mother of God', and whispered confessions to the priest who would then dish out absolution to the penitent soul. The places of worship soon changed with increased wealth in Christendom and the idea of a 'priesthood of all believers' (cf. 1 Peter 2:9) was soon forgotten with the professional priest now regarded as of a different order from the laity and as having a special grace and divine authority by reason of his ordination. The altar at which he officiated and upon which he offered again and again the sacrifice of the body and blood of Christ, came to be regarded as the most sacred place in the building and was railed off from the nave of the church. Thus, there grew up a priestly caste separated from the people.

4) The establishment and spread of Islam

During the Middle Ages, the rise of Islam posed a significant challenge to Christianity – a challenge that continues until this day. The Prophet Muhammad was born in Mecca, Arabia, in about 570 AD and at an early age lost his parents. When he grew to manhood, he prayed much in the solitudes of the desert, fell into trances and claimed that he heard voices. He began to meet both Jews and those who would profess to be 'Christian' but had only a false version of the Gospels and while they gave Muhammad the idea that there was but one God, he was not at all impressed by their lives. This may have 'prevented him from becoming a Christian.'[22] He resolved to replace the degraded polytheism, prevalent in Arabia at that time, by the one and true religion of Allah, whose prophet he claimed to be.

Owing to the intense opposition to his preaching, he had to flee from Mecca in 622 AD and went with some two hundred of his followers to Medina, some 200 miles away. This *Hegira*, as the flight was called, was the turning point in his career and from it the Muslim era is dated. Nine years later he re-entered Mecca in triumph and by the time of his death in 632 AD 'he had won over all Arabia'[23] with his teaching. Such teaching continued and within only 80 years after his death, Islam (meaning 'submission') stretched all the way from India in the East to the Atlantic in the West. Soon it penetrated into Central Asia and parts of China, stretching through South Asia to Malaya. In the great 'Christian' cities of Antioch, Jerusalem and Alexandria in Egypt, only remnants of the Christian Church remained. In Syria alone, 10,000 churches were destroyed or transformed into mosques and the powerful Church of North Africa - with its memories of Kingdom-greats such as Tertullian, Cyprian, Origen and Augustine – was practically obliterated until only small Christian communities survived here and there. Today, conservative figures number followers of Muhammad at 1.6 billion adherents. It begs the question, how different the picture could have been had the young prophet, during his early years of quest, encountered genuine Christ-followers, both possessing and proclaiming the true gospel of Jesus.

Lights in the darkness

Although medieval times were undeniably an age of change and decay for the Church, there were some 'bright lights' and a clear testimony to the fact that Jesus' Church would be built despite the forces that opposed it. Influential characters during this time include:

The Venerable Bede (born c. 672 AD)

'The Father of English History' – this is how the prolific author and scholar, Saint Bede is described due to his most famous work, *the Ecclesiastic History of the English Church and People.* The Venerable Bede[24] was born in either 672 or 673 AD near Jarrow, Northumbria to well-to-do parents. At the age of 7, Bede was sent to the monastery of Monkwearmouth by his family to be educated by Benedict Biscop and later to the sister monastery at Jarrow under Ceolfrith. In 686 AD, a devastating plague broke out at Jarrow and records from that time state that only two surviving monks were capable of singing the full offices – one was Ceolfrith and the other a young boy, most probably Bede himself who would have been 13 or 14 at the time.

The young monk showed great promise and at the tender age of 19, he was ordained a deacon by the Bishop of Hexham. The canonical age for the ordination of a deacon was 25 – proof, no doubt, of Bede's considerably abilities. His ordination to the priesthood came at the age of 30 and this was performed by the same Bishop of Hexham. In about 701 AD Bede wrote his first works and continued to write for the rest of his life, eventually completing over 60 books, most of which have survived but often difficult to date. These include translations of various books of the Bible, Scripture commentaries, theological and historical works as well as scientific and musical documents. In addition to writing, Bede was a teacher, an accomplished singer and reciter of poetry – all the more interesting as there is evidence that he suffered from a speech impediment during times of his life. He was certainly no stranger to controversy and at one point he was regarded by some local monks as a 'heretic' due to his calculations that Christ was born 3,952 years after the creation of the world. The standard theological view accepted by theologians at the time was 'over 5000 years'. There is also evidence from Bede's own writings that he was married – with various references to a wife. Very unusual for a monk both then and now!

Bede died on Thursday, 26th May 735 AD which was 'Ascension Day', on the floor of his cell, singing *Glory be to the Father and to the Son and to the Holy Spirit*. In the hours before his death, he had been dictating to a scribe and had distributed the last of his money and possessions to fellow monks. Except for a few visits to other monasteries, including the one at Lindisfarne, or Holy Island, his life was spent mainly in prayer, observance of the monastic discipline as well as the study, teaching and writing of Scripture. He was considered the most learned man of his time,[25] though he seemed also to be a man of the Spirit. In his famous *History of the English Church and People* he mentions several miracles, including storms that were stilled after prayer, miraculous healings and even those who were raised from the dead. Such accounts give evidence of the continued use of spiritual gifts long after the time of the 1st century Apostolic Age.

Abbess Hildegard (b. 1098 AD)
'A feather on the breath of God' – that is how one of the most versatile, colourful and gifted women of the Middle Ages modestly

described herself. Abbess Hildegard of Bingen was the founder and first abbess of the Benedictine community of Bingen on the Rhine in Germany. Although she did not begin to write until the age of 43, Hildegard became a prolific and diverse writer, her works including a massive trilogy that combines Christian doctrine and ethics with cosmology, or the origin of the universe, an encyclopaedia of medicine and natural sciences, a correspondence comprising of several hundred letters to people from every stratus of society, a body of exquisite music that includes some seventy liturgical songs and the first known morality play. An astounding achievement considering that as far as Hildegard knew, no woman had ever written before.

Abbess Hildegard is also notable for her charismatic activity. On occasions she spoken in a *lingua ignota* or unknown tongue and recorded such words in a dictionary which comprised over a thousand entries. In addition, similar to some of her contemporaries such as Joachim of Fiore and Francis of Assisi, from the tender age of three or four she is said to have received several visions during her lifetime, 26 of which form her most significant work, *Scivias*, which took some ten years to complete. In her latter years she became an advisor to princes and popes and from the age of 60 until her death at 81, she undertook preaching tours on which she called for reform of the Church. A full life indeed!

Although in some eyes, both the substance and the style of Hildegard's teaching can be viewed as unpalatable in places - for example, many modern Protestants would find her eulogies of Mary and her picturesque and sometimes complex visions unacceptable - in recent years there has been an increased interest in this 12th century mystic. The reasons for this could include her gender, her role as a female leader and because part of her message echoes some of our own contemporary concerns such as for the environment or 'Green' issues. It should be remembered that Hildegard lived and ministered in a time of turbulence, squabbling and wars in the name of Christ,[26] where spiritual gifts, as we would know and experience them today, were scarce, where the Church was corrupt and where the heavens seemed as brass. She sought to be open and available to communicate something of the heart of God to her generation - by the power of the Spirit, through her music, visions and writing.

Francis of Assisi (born c. 1181 AD)

'The best-loved of the medieval saints' – this is how Tony Lane describes Francis of Assisi.[27] Francis was born at the end of the 12th century to a wealthy merchant in Italy. His life before his early twenties was spent in pursuit of worldly pleasures until a number of 'God-encounters' led him to pursue a life of simplicity, poverty and contemplation. The story is told that whilst praying in a ruined church building outside of his native Assisi, he heard a voice telling him to rebuild God's house. This he started to do physically, though later realising that the command was to build the Kingdom in a spiritual sense! In his zeal he sold some of his father's materials in order to raise money for the building project. When his father found out he was incensed and proceeded to march the young Francis to the local bishop in order to claim back what he had lost. From that moment on, the young man vowed that his heavenly Father alone would be his provider and he began a nomadic life of travelling and poverty based on Matthew 10:7-10. Disciples soon began to gather around him and after writing the now-lost *Primitive Rule*, he entered Rome and presented his work to the pope at that time, Innocent III. In 1212 Francis was joined by Clare, a young lady from a privileged background and with his help, she founded the 'Poor Clares' – a female version of the Franciscan Order. Francis continued writing, producing *First Rule* and *Second Rule* and, in 1224, while praying on Mount Alverna, he received the 'stigmata' or the five wounds of Christ. Francis died two years later in 1226.

Francis' life was marked by a ministry of preaching a simple message of devotion to Jesus – a message energised by a deep concern for the poor and the outcast, which resulted in the establishing of orphanages and hospitals. He is also called 'the first missionary to the Muslim world'[28] with numerous, though largely unsuccessful, attempts to evangelise the Saracens. His biographer, St. Bonaventure, also portrays Francis as a man of the Spirit and various accounts of spiritual encounters and both the ability to discern the hidden motives of people's heart and to have insight into events before they happened are documented.

Other voices

In addition to Bede, Hildegard and Francis, others throughout the Middle Ages were stirred by the Spirit to become latter-day John-the-Baptists, those who would cry out in the wilderness and against the established Church of their day. These include Pierre Valdez, or Peter Waldo, from the late 12th and early 13th century. Valdez had renounced his earthly wealth to pursue a ministry of preaching, prayer and Bible translation and after careful study of the Scriptures, both he and his followers, conscious of how far the Church had deviated from the clear teaching of the New Testament, began to speak out. Despite opposition, the Waldensians flourished in several parts of Europe at that time and a clear example of 'a Protestant church some three centuries before the Reformation'[29] can be seen.

Joachim of Fiore can be described as one of the most fascinating figures of the Middle Ages. After a pilgrimage to the Holy Land in the 12th century he devoted himself to the ministry and entered a monastery. Although he was later appointed as the leader of a Cistercian monastery at Curazzo in Southern Italy, his desire was for the study of the Scriptures and in particular to understand the Book of Revelation in addition to other prophetic writings. He founded his own monastery that gained papal approval and soon leaders, both spiritual and secular, approached him for advice. These include Pope Lucius III and Richard the Lion Heart, the latter enquiring as to his chances against Saladin during the Crusades at that time.

It is interesting to note that during the medieval period, some operated the gifts of the Spirit as listed by Paul in 1 Corinthians 12 proving that such gifts did not, in fact, cease with the 1st century Church, but have continued to this very day. In addition to the charismatic[30] practices of Bede, Abbess Hildegard and Francis, John of Beverley (d. 721 AD) exercised a remarkable ministry of healing, both St Antony of Padua (d. 1231) and St Vincent Ferrer (d. 1419) spoke in other tongues and St. Francis Xavier (d. 1552) is said to have spoke in tongues, healed the sick and established communities of Christians in the Far East.

From the examples of individuals given in this chapter it was clear that by the 14th and 15th centuries, serious 'cracks' were starting to appear in the Roman Catholic Church – the final sledgehammer blow came through what was later known as The Reformation.

CHAPTER 5   REFORMATION IN EUROPE

'The Lord said to Moses, 'I have indeed seen the misery of my people...go, I am sending you..' (Exod. 3:7a, 10a)

By the early 16th century, the Pope's rule over Christendom appeared secure. The Roman Catholic Church was experiencing growth and expansion with several 'successful' missions to spread Christianity to the Americas, African and the Far East and various attempts to give overall power to a general council rather than the Holy See had failed.[31] At this time, the Church possessed vast wealth and was massively influential – maintaining control over every area of a person's life from the cradle to the grave. However, this perceived security was soon to be shaken to its very core and foundations by an 'earthquake' later known as the Protestant Reformation.

A number of factors paved the way for this reformation. The late medieval papacy amply illustrated the maxim that absolute power corrupts absolutely. Allen states how the lifestyles of some of the higher clergy were a 'disgrace to their holy calling'[32] with tales of incest and illegitimate children. According to Geikie, 'it was the fashion to call into question the very principles of Christianity'.[33] Parish priests were poorly educated and many lazy in carrying out their tasks. With the rise in the sense of nationality, people began to resent the foreign rule of Rome and they begrudged paying tithes to build magnificent cathedrals and personal residences for clergy at HQ, whilst their own individual churches saw little or no improvement. There was a resurgence of interest in Humanism and in Southern Europe there was a focus on the pagan Greek and Roman classics. The different monastic orders began to bicker with each other and on more than one occasion rival popes fought for supreme power.

In addition the invention of the printing press by Gutenberg in 1456 was a major catalyst in the major change that was coming– enabling the Scriptures and other protestant literature to be available to the masses. Upon reading the New Testament, many became aware of how far the Church of Rome had deviated away from the clear teaching of the Bible. This began an age of questioning and rethinking on true doctrine and practice and voices began to cry out in the wilderness.

It would be fair to say that reformation was beginning to take place in parts of Europe long before the well-documented events and characters of the 16th century. The efforts of such people as John Wycliffe (b. 1320) with the translation of Scripture into the language of the people, and Czech priest Jan Hus (b. 1369) who dared to speak out against the religious leadership of his day, are worthy of note. However, it took a century more before a modern-day 'Moses' was raised up to deliver God's people from the oppression of the times – Martin Luther.

Martin Luther – 'Here I stand'

Luther was born in Eisleben, Saxony on the 10th November, 1483. His father was a miner and town councillor who wanted young Martin to study law in order to enter the legal profession. At his father's insistence, he entered university in 1501 where he became an earnest and music-loving student. After graduating with an M.A. in 1505, Martin was deeply moved by the sudden death of a friend and after a narrow escape from lightening he decided to enter an Augustinian monastery in Erfurt in search of salvation. The monastery had earned respect under the supervision of Johann von Staupitz and in the time that followed Luther sought God and truth through a variety of means including fasting, recited prayer, scourging his body and freezing himself in an unheated cubicle. Luther later summarised this time by stating:

'If ever a monk got into heaven by monkery,
I should have gotten there....'[34]

During this time Luther read one of Jan Hus' tracts which deeply touched him. He exclaimed:

'I wondered why a man who could write so Christianly
and powerfully had been burned...I shut the book
and turned away with a wounded heart.'[35]

Luther soon advanced and went to Wittenberg at the command of his superiors for a future professorship. He received his Bachelor of Theology degree in 1509 and was chosen to go to Rome on pilgrimage where he went through every pilgrim devotion possible, eventually climbing the stone steps of Santa Scala on his bare knees. He earned so many indulgences that he almost wished his parents dead so he could deliver them from purgatory![36] The corruption and immorality of Rome horrified him enough to describe it as 'an abomination' when the papal court was served at supper by six naked girls.

Luther was made a Doctor of Divinity in 1512 and he began to lecture at the new Wittenburg University and was licensed to preach, eventually being made a District Vicar over eleven monasteries. Despite such achievements the young priest and academic had no peace and his sense of sin overwhelmed him at times. The kindly Staupitz sought to help Luther by pointing out that true penitence begins not with fear of a punishing God but with a healthy fear of a loving God. Other colleagues helped further by giving the young friar what was then a rare personal possession – a Latin Bible.

Luther's study of the Scriptures opened up altogether new truths for him. He began to see that many of the doctrines of the Church that he had held since birth and even taught to others had no basis in Scripture. By the time he began to lecture on Psalms between 1513-1515, he was convinced that salvation was a new relationship with God, based not on *trying* and human effort, but through *trusting* – faith in the finished work of Christ. From the study of the Apostle Paul's writings, Luther was convinced that salvation was in essence a right relationship with God and from Romans in particular his confidence turned to conviction that that godly faith gave personal assurance. From that time on, the Gospel was forgiveness of sins, 'good news' that filled the soul with peace, joy and absolute trust in God.[37]

During this time, a silver-tongued Dominican monk by the name of John Tetzel (1470-1519) came to town. Tetzel's brief was to raise money for the Church in Rome and to do this he spoke about indulgences in a way never heard before. An indulgence, or 'papal pardon' could be bought that when cashed-in would result in less time spent in purgatory[38] for oneself or a loved one. The sales technique of Tetzel soon resulted in a jingle or proverb:

> *'When a coin in the coffer rings, a soul*
> *from purgatory springs.'*

Such propaganda infuriated Luther who was convinced that only a right relationship with God, through Christ, brought salvation – a free gift and not through the payment of silver or gold (see 1 Peter 1:18). In response, as was the custom of the day, in 1517, on the door of the church at Wittenburg University, Luther nailed his '95 Theses', challenging to public debate all he found false in this and other church practices. Tetzel felt compelled to answer with his own '106 Anti-Theses' – an act that only served to add fuel to the fire.

By 1517, the message of Luther, and other reformers, was clear and contained at least three vital components that make up the basic framework of Protestant belief:

1) A person is justified, or made right with a holy God, by faith alone, or *Sola Fide*;

2) Each believer has access to God directly and not through a human go-between. All true believers are priests, thus what became known as *the priesthood of all believers*;[39]

3) The *Bible* is the supreme source of authority for both faith and life or *Sola Scriptura*.

Luther soon circulated his ideas and thoughts amongst the university network in his nation. However, what was designed to be a fairly local and academic debate, soon turned into both a national and international controversy that rocked the whole of Christendom at the time and its aftermath felt since. Luther was soon joined by the brilliant yet frail and shy, young Greek scholar - Phillip Melanchthon. Tracts and books were soon published and distributed and Luther's pen became prolific. In work after work, he questioned the Pope's supreme power, the validity of various Church practices and he argued for the 'Paper Pope' – the written Scriptures as the final authority in all matters of faith and doctrine. Through Gutenberg's printing press Luther's ideas spread far and wide and soon others, including Ulrich Zwingli and John Calvin, joined the attack.

It was inevitable that with such vocal and widespread criticism of the antics of the Roman Church, the full imposing might of a papal council was called against Luther. He was summoned to a Diet, or Council, at Worms in 1521 where a recantation of his views would be demanded. Although like Christ in Gethsemane when many of his friends abandoned him, Luther 'set his face like a flint' and faced his accusers stating:

> *'If there be as many devils at Worms as tiles*
> *on the roof-tops I will enter.'[40]*

During the trial, Luther was asked to retract his controversial writings and views. Almost succumbing to the pressure of the occasion he requested time to think and the next day when the council reconvened, although acknowledging his forthright style, he replied in German:

> '*Unless I am convicted by the testimony of Sacred Scripture*
> *or by evident reason....my conscious is captive to the*
> *Word of God. I cannot and will not recant anything for*
> *to go against my conscience is neither right nor safe.*
> *Here I stand, I can do no other. So help me God....'[41]*

The packed audience applauded and although condemned to death by the state, Luther was abducted on the way to his sentence by King Frederick the Wise who hid him in his castle in Wartburg. Here, in exile, Martin was able to continue writing including a translation of the Bible in German. He eventually died in 1548 from exposure after a cold, January journey in an attempt to reconcile two friends who had quarrelled. On his death-bed, he was heard to quote John 3:16. His body was buried in the Castle Church in Wittenburg and his memorial engraved with some of the words spoken at his trial in Worms.

Summary

Although Luther is arguably one of the few men of whom it may be said that the history of the world was profoundly altered by his work – there are certainly some negatives from the period of the Reformation era and from the Reformers themselves. These include the harsh treatment of the Anabaptists,[42] Luther's anti-Semitic views, his violent disagreements with other reformers such as Zwingli over the doctrine of the Lord's Supper, the retention of the practice of infant baptism and the reformer's general skepticism of spiritual gifts and supernatural miracles - to name but a few.

However, despite such human failings, the turning-point event of 1517 and its aftermath resulted in a seismic shift for the Church in Europe and beyond. By the time of Luther's death, the Protestant Reformation with its various branches including Reformed, Lutheran and Anglican - took hold in countries such as Germany, Switzerland, Holland, Scandinavia, France and also Great Britain, where we turn our attention to next.

CHAPTER 6   THE FIRST GREAT AWAKENING – WESLEY AND WHITEFIELD

'Then I heard the voice of the Lord saying, 'Whom shall I send? And who will go for us?'' (Isaiah 6:8)

Britain in the mid-17th to mid-18th century was in a state of moral and spiritual decline. According to Arnold Dallimore, the so-called 'Gin Craze' began in 1689 and within a generation every sixth house became a gin shop. The poor were unspeakably wretched – over 160 crimes had the death penalty and alcohol made the people what they were never before – cruel and inhuman. Hanging was a daily gala event and prisons were a living 'hell' where both young and old, first-time offender and seasoned criminal were thrown together to fight for survival in filthy surroundings. Women were badly treated with many turning to prostitution and theft to provide for their children.[43]

In addition to such corruption, a movement called *Deism*[44] became popular at this time and its emphasis on rationalising everything, including the Bible, the Virgin Birth, the Resurrection of Christ and miracles, saw many growing cold towards the Church, believing Christianity to be false and irrelevant. As was the case before the Reformation, large numbers viewed the Christian faith as a ritual instead of a living relationship and empty formality became the order of the day.

Thus, in the decade between 1730 and 1740, life in England was morally corrupt and deeply crippled by spiritual decay. Yet, among such conditions a revival or 'Great Awakening' broke out that touched not only Britain but also other parts of the world. God's main instruments at this time were two men, namely John Wesley and George Whitefield.

John Wesley – A 'Brand Plucked From The Burning' (Zech. 3:2)

John Wesley was born on the 17th June 1703 to Anglican clergyman, Samuel, and his wife Suzanna. In 1709 the parsonage in Epworth, Lincolnshire, where the Wesley family lived, caught on fire and burned to the ground in only 15 minutes. Whilst Samuel was helping his other children over the wall to safety, he could hear the cries of his six-year old son who was still in the inferno in the upstairs of the house. Although Samuel attempted to re-enter the parsonage, the fierce flames drove him back and with other members of his family, they knelt and prayed that God may receive John's soul. However, unbeknown to them, whilst the young John was crying for help, a man from the village was helped up to the window and the boy leapt into his arms and then taken to his surprised, yet overjoyed parents. From this time onwards, the young Wesley felt that he was rescued for a purpose and whilst in his teens, he followed in his father's footsteps and trained for the Anglican ministry at Oxford University. After ordination in 1728, John returned to Epworth where he worked alongside his father before returning to Oxford, this time as a tutor. John's younger brother, Charles, was himself a student at this time and with a group of like-minded individuals, had started to meet in his chambers for prayer, study of the Scriptures, the taking of Holy Communion and for the co-ordination of outreach to the local prisons. Due to their methodical approach, the group was nicknamed the 'Holy Club' or 'Methodists' by the other students and it was this group that John joined on his return to university.[45]

By early 1736, John was on board a ship bound for the new colonies in America to undertake missionary service. After settling in the new colony of Georgia he met a Moravian[46] pastor, August Spangenberg, who asked the young missionary, 'Do you know

Jesus Christ?'[47] and who challenged him towards a personal faith in the Saviour. In 1738, after some two years of 'ministry', Wesley returned to Britain feeling an utter failure. He recorded in his diary:

> *'I went to America to convert the Indians,*
> *but oh, who shall convert me?'[48]*

Thus began a quest for personal salvation and after prayer, searching the Scripture and consultation with others, the pilgrimage finally ended when, some three months after his return to Britain, Wesley found himself in a little Aldersgate prayer meeting, listening to Luther's *Preface to the Romans* being read. His *Journals* describe this momentous occasion on Wednesday May 24th, 1738:

> *'About a quarter to nine, while he was describing the*
> *change which God works in the heart through faith in*
> *Christ, I felt my heart strangely warmed. I felt I did trust*
> *Christ, Christ alone for salvation; and an assurance was*
> *given me that He had take away my sins, even mine,*
> *and saved me from the law of sin and death.'[49]*

His joy was further increased when he soon learned that his brother, Charles, who went on to become a prolific hymn writer and penning some 6000 songs, had accepted Christ only three days earlier.

John Wesley soon continued preaching with a new vigour and for three months visited the Moravians in Germany. On his return although pulpits in the Anglican Church began to close to him, he began aggressive measures to evangelise in England and after taking advice from his 'Holy Club' friend and colleague, George Whitefield, Wesley began to preach in the open air – wherever and whenever God gave him an audience. Thus began the ministry of a man who rose daily at 4.00am, was preaching at 5.00am so working men could attend services and who, during the next fifty-two years, traveled some 225,000 miles, mostly on horseback, preached over 50,000 sermons, wrote hymns and penned close to 233 books on a range of subjects – including an early text on electricity! 'Never', says Ryle, 'did any man have so many irons in the fire at one time and yet succeed in keeping so many hot'.[50]Up and down the breadth of Britain, despite much opposition by both the churched and un-churched, people were converted in their thousands and such converts were nurtured by means of the Methodist societies that were set up by Wesley and his followers – meetings that sought to teach, pray and encourage – similar to the earlier meetings at Oxford. Although John and Charles both remained loyal members of the Church of England until their deaths, it was clear that a new movement was bursting forth and 'by the 1780s, the Methodists were effectively a separate body from the Anglicans.'[51]

John Wesley preached for sixty-five years, dying finally at 88 with the words: 'The best of all, God is with us' and the first words of the hymn 'I'll praise my Maker while I've breath.' He left behind him 750 preachers in England and 350 in American, 76,968 Methodists in England and 57,621 in America

What was John Wesley's contribution to the Church both then and since? Howard Snyder's research on Wesley highlights the evangelist's organisational ability, his discipline, his community principles as well as his reliance on spiritual power to accomplish God's work.[52] Others would point to Methodism's influence on 19th century evangelicalism – including the British and Foreign Bible Society and the Church Missionary Society and Wilberforce's effect upon society, including the abolition of slavery. However, according to some, one of Wesley's greatest contributions was his teaching on 'the second blessing', which opened the door the way for belief in a subsequent work of the Holy Spirit after conversion.

Although Wesley was generally 'cessationist'[53] rather than 'continuationist' in his view on spiritual gifts, favouring character or fruit instead of the *charismata*, there was an emphasis in his teaching on the Holy Spirit regarding a further endowment of grace. This he sometimes called 'perfect love' or 'entire sanctification,' otherwise known as 'the second blessing'. Such an endowment of the Spirit would enable the believer to live a life devoted to God and be empowered for His service. Although some at the time, and others since, have wished to call this the 'baptism in the Holy Spirit' as taught in such New Testament passages as Matt. 3:11, Wesley was generally opposed to using such a term. Despite such reluctance, however, the 'second blessing' teaching of Wesley and the Methodists after him did pave the way for the expectation of another work of the Spirit after conversion, an expectation picked up by the 19th century Holiness churches and developed by 20th century Pentecostals[54] into the biblical doctrine of a Spirit-baptism post-conversion for the purpose of witnessing (cf. Acts 1:8) and evidenced by spiritual gifts, especially speaking in other tongues.

George Whitefield – A prince of preachers

Another of God's instruments, used to preserve the corrupt society of 18th century Britain, was George Whitefield. Ryle states:

> *'Of all the spiritual heroes of the time, none saw so soon as Whitefield what the times demanded and none were so forward in the great work of spiritual aggression.'[55]*

Although Whitefield and Wesley were friends and colleagues, they couldn't have been more different – in up-bringing, theology, mannerisms and style. As a boy, the young George was a self-confessed liar, thief, gambler and mimic who was raised in a hotel tavern in Gloucester called the 'Bell Inn'. For the first sixteen years of his life he grew up amongst highwaymen, who planned their attacks at the bar room tables, and pimps who plied their trade among the many customers. It was in these surroundings that the soon-to-be evangelist developed both a vivid imagination and a voice that was soon to become so powerful and expressive that in the open air it was rumoured that his words could carry for five miles and thousands could hear him! It was said the top actor of the day, David Garrick, would often make time in his busy schedule to hear the great evangelist speak and once stated that he would give 100 guineas to be able to say 'Oh!' like Whitefield.

Whitefield's childhood home was a broken one, with poverty, disillusionment and a stepfather and mother who finally separated. At the age of 17, the young George was sent off to Oxford to make something of himself and to contemplate his future. It was here, in 1733, that he met Charles Wesley who invited him to the newly founded 'Holy Club'. Although such a club was arguably a vain attempt by the Wesleys and other members to become better people it did cause George to seek truth and after reading Henry Scougal's *The Life of God in the Soul of a Man,* he exclaimed:

> 'God showed me I must be born again or be damned! I
> learned a man may go to church, say his prayers, receive
> the sacraments and yet not be a Christian.'[56]

Unfortunately, such a 'revelation' did not instil faith but fear, with Whitefield embarking on a form of asceticism[57] where he would wear patched clothes, dirty shoes, eat vile food and lay prostrate on the floor for days on end in the pursuit of peace with God. Such a quest continued for almost a year, during which time the pressure almost drove him to despair, ruined his studies and cost him his place in the Holy Club. Finally, after exhausting all human resources, God revealed himself to Whitefield. He states:

> 'God was pleased to remove the heavy load, to enable
> me to lay hold of His dear Son by a living faith,

and by giving me the Spirit of adoption, to seal me
even to the day of everlasting redemption.'[58]

Shortly after this momentous event, Whitefield preached his first sermon at the age of 21 to a congregation of some 300 people, including Robert Raikes, the founder of the Sunday School. Thus began the 'preaching that startled the nation' and, as Ryle continues, Whitefield:

'Obtained a degree of popularity such as no preacher or
since has probably every reached....No preacher has ever
been so universally popular in every country he visited,
in England, Scotland and America. No preacher has ever
retained his hold on his hearers so entirely as he did for
34 years. His popularity never waned. It was as great at
the end of his days as it was at the beginning.....'[59]

Wherever and whenever Whitefield preached the churches were crowded – such an eloquent orator who preached the pure Gospel with a varying use of voice and mannerisms was at that time a novelty in Britain. He literally took the nation by storm! He attracted listeners from all walks of life – rich and poor, the educated and ignorant, the famous and ordinary. Literary men such as Lord Bolingbroke and Lord Chesterfield were frequently found in his audience with the former declaring, 'He is the most extraordinary man in our times with the most commanding eloquence I ever heard in any person'. The eminent polymath and one of the Founding Fathers of the United States, Benjamin Franklin spoke enthusiastically of Whitefield's preaching powers and David Hume, the Scottish philosopher and historian, stated how 'it was worth riding twenty miles to hear him'.

From the occasion of his first sermon to his final breath at the relatively young age of 56, Whitefield worked tirelessly – similar to his friend and colleague, John Wesley. He usually rose at 4.00am and would spend whole nights in reading and devotions. He preached morning, afternoon and evening on Sundays, 6.00 every morning and evening Monday to Thursday and Saturday night – on average some twelve messages a week and sometimes forty to sixty hours of speaking per week. In addition, he would carry out correspondence with people in almost every part of the world. In his thirty-four years of ministry he visited almost every town in England, Scotland and Wales, crossed the Atlantic seven times and publicly preached an estimated 18,000 messages. However, none of the 75 recorded sermons attributed to Whitefield do him justice. Although they were penned in shorthand and are terribly disjointed and dismembered, this 'Prince of Preachers' communicated extremely simply, was bold, direct and full of the Gospel. He dramatised his speech and actions so vividly that sermons seemed to move and walk before the listeners' eyes and he was never seen to get through one single message without a tear – he felt deeply for the souls before him.

Under Wesley's request, Whitefield went to the colony of Georgia, in what is now known as the United States, for a year to help with Savannah Orphan House. On his return to Britain he found that the majority of his Anglican colleagues were no longer favourable to him due to Whitefield's forthright preaching on the need to be 'born again'. When pulpits began to close to the young preacher, he turned his efforts to the open-air – a radical idea at that time! His first attempt was among the Kingswood colliers near Bristol in February of 1739. He began to speak on a hill[60] to about one or two hundred coal miners on their way to and from work. Whitefield wrote in his journals of how he noticed the sight of the white gutters made by the miners' tears, which fell plentifully down their black cheeks as they came out of the coal-pits. Word soon spread and Whitefield's audience increased and multiplied until on occasions, even in the wind, rain and snow, some 20,000 workers would stand and listen to the dynamic young preacher who would captivate them with no gimmicks, no flashing lights and no microphone!

Whitefield's sole purpose was outreach, to preach Christ and to exhort men, women, boys and girls to repent and be saved. His Calvinistic belief persuaded him that there were those in each audience who were not far from the Kingdom and ready to be saved. The results and fruit of his preaching were astonishing. In one single week of preaching in the Moorfields area of London, a district well known for its brothels, crime and poverty, Whitefield received one thousand letters from people under spiritual conviction and some 350 were admitted to communion.

After some thirty-one years of selfless service, Whitefield died as suddenly as he had lived. During one of his U.S. tours at Newbury Port, Massachusetts he was taken ill after a single spasmodic fit of asthma. Though ill and tired, he preached his last open-air sermon the day before his death on September 29th 1770. He later prayed, 'Lord Jesus, I am weary in Thy work but not of Thy work'. He ate with a friend and after retiring to his bedroom, tradition states that he passed away in his sleep. 'Sudden death', he would often say, is 'Sudden glory!'

From Whitefield we learn this: God can use anyone who loves enough to care and cares enough to give their life totally to His service. God is looking for someone He can trust with His Gospel.

Whilst the Lord was at work in the British Isles, a Second Great Awakening was breaking out on the other side of the Atlantic – in North America.

CHAPTER 7   THE SECOND GREAT AWAKENING - THE OTHER SIDE OF THE 'POND'

'The earth will be filled with the knowledge of the glory of the Lord as the waters cover the sea.' (Hab. 2:14)

By the early 19th century, the Church in the newly-created United States of America was experiencing doctrinal division, party politics and the influence of Thomas Paine's *Age of Reason* which promoted Deism, rejected miracles and questioned the legitimacy of the Bible. As Pratney states, 'The effect on U.S. Colleges was disastrous'[61] with rebellion against society and rationalism becoming the order of the day. Disturbingly, it was not only secular universities that were affected. Bible Colleges, themselves, became centres of skepticism, many held mock communion services, some forced the resignation of its President and one Bible College attempted to blow up a campus building! Although most true believing college students began to meet in secret in order to keep their faith, some college preachers came to the fore and began to see conviction spreading amongst fellow-students as they counter-attacked the rebellion with powerful sermons, preached under great anointing.

At the same time, in other parts of the United States, revival fire was starting to blaze, especially on the pioneer frontiers of Kentucky, through two North Carolina Presbyterian ministers, James McGready and his protégé, Barton Stone.

Red River and Cane Ridge - Frontier fire!

James McGready was a country preacher, pastor and fervent man of prayer. In mid-1800 he called on the people of Southern Kentucky to gather for a four-day breaking of bread service and many gathered on the edge of the prairie at Red River expecting blessing. Witnesses described the scenes as 'baffling description with very many falling down as though slain in battle, with those in a motionless state who soon exhibited symptoms of life by deep groans or piercing shrieks.'[62] Friday and Saturday saw floods of repentant tears and then times of exuberant rejoicing. The climax came on the final day when John McGee, a local Methodist minister gave the closing address. He describes, in his own words, the response:

> *'I exhorted them to let the Lord omnipotent reign in their hearts and to submit to Him and their souls should live...I turned again and losing sight of the fear of man, I went through the house shouting and exhorting with all possible ecstasy and energy and the floor was soon covered by the slain.'[63]*

People attended the meetings at Red River from a 100-mile radius and due to a lack of local accommodation they bought bedding and tents for temporary housing. Thus, the first camp meeting was born.

According to McGready, none of the attendees wanted to go home and both hunger and sleep seemed to affect nobody. Temporary concerns paled into insignificance compared to the eternal blessings that were being received. The revival seemed to touch people from every walk of life including college professors and farmers, male and female, black and white:

*'Persons of every description were to be found
in every part of the multitude crying out for
mercy in the most extreme distress.'[64]*

One of the leaders who was greatly affected by the Red River revival was Barton Stone who returned home and called for similar meetings to be held in Bourbon County at Cane Ridge. In May 1801 meetings were attended with great blessing and a second gathering was held in August of the same year where over 20,000 attended for six days of camp meetings. A witness described the scenes:

*'The notice was like the roar of Niagara. I counted seven
ministers, all preaching at the same time, some on tree
stumps, some in wagons and one from a tree. Some people
were singing, others praying, some crying for mercy.
At one time I saw at least five hundred swept down in
a moment as if a battery of a thousand guns had been
opened up upon them. This was immediately followed
by shrieks and shouts that rent the very heavens.'[65]*

Similar scenes were witnessed across other parts of the United States and the American frontier was soon set ablaze with mainstream denominations such as the Presbyterians, Methodists and Baptists all catching revival 'fire.' Through the camp meeting approach the eastern part of the United States was radically transformed. Instead of gambling, cursing and vice, true Christian spirituality became the dominant feature of the day. According to Pratney:

*'It was God's great hour. Revival stopped skepticism
in its tracks and returned the helm of the country*

to the godly.'[66]

Emerging from this new 'move of God' was the Methodist circuit rider, Peter Cartwright and the revivalist, Charles Grandison Finney.

Peter Cartwright – 'God's Plowman'

Peter Cartwright was born in Amherst County, Virginia in 1785 and at age 5 his father, a veteran of the Revolutionary War, moved his family west to Kentucky. Cartwright received little schooling during his childhood though he soon became adept as a gambler at cards and horse racing in his teenage years. This, however, came to an abrupt end after the prayers and pleading of his godly mother, when he was converted during a camp meeting in the Great Western Revival in 1801. He joined the Methodist Church and was soon licensed as a lay speaker. In 1802, a year after his conversion and at the age of 17, he was commissioned to form a new circuit[67] of preaching posts in the unchurched frontier wilderness around the mouth of the Cumberland River. Here began a frontier ministry that lasted over 60 years in both northern and southern states and that saw Cartwright personally baptizing an estimated 12,000 converts during this time. He preached to hosts of men and women, speaking for three hours at a stretch, several times a week. The conviction in his booming voice 'could make women weep and strong men tremble'[68] and thousands responded to the gospel in meetings that lasted day and night. Several church buildings were erected to house services for the new converts.

Cartwright sought to mix his frontier preaching with politics and in 1824, he moved to Sangamon County, Illinois. He entered politics in order to oppose slavery and served several terms in the lower house of the Illinois general assembly. It was here that he was defeated for a seat in Congress in 1846 by a young Abraham Lincoln who eventually became the 16th president of the United States from 1861 until his assassination in 1865.

A colourful, yet tough character, Cartwright was a straight-talker[69] and knew regular hardships throughout his ministry. He experienced floods, thieves, hunger and disease in on the brutal frontier, yet met every challenge head on. He learned to deal with those who sought to disrupt his meetings, he often went days without food when on the circuit and once returned home after several weeks away with only 6 cents of borrowed money in his pocket. His father had to outfit him with new clothes, saddle and a horse before he could ride again. Despite his poverty, Cartwright married and raised children. However, his family were not spared tragedy. Forced to camp in the open one night, they were startled awake when a tree snapped in two; Cartwright raised his arms to deflect the falling log, but it crushed his youngest daughter to death.

Peter Cartwright died at the age of 87 near Pleasant Plains, Illinois leaving behind an autobiography which was published in 1856. His courage and tenacity in the face of danger won him many sons and daughters for Christ. It was said of him – 'He stayed at his post to do his duty'.

Charles G. Finney – 'For such a time as this'
Charles Finney was born in Warren, Connecticut a year after John Wesley died, in 1792, and thus proved to be a link between the 1st and 2nd Great Awakenings. He was a tall, impressive-looking young frontiersman from a farming family who possessed a quick sense of humour, a zest for life, was an able musician, expert marksman and successful athlete – without equal. Although Finney was not raised in a Christian home, he regularly attended a local Presbyterian church, though he often scorned the prayer meetings because 'he never saw any of their prayers answered.' It was here that he met his first wife, Lydia and the young Finney started training to become a lawyer. During his law studies, he

was struck by the number of times one of his college text books referred to the Bible as the basis for all civil and moral law. After a period of searching and under deep conviction from Scripture, he vowed one October Sunday evening in the Autumn of 1821 to 'settle the question of salvation once and for all.'[73]

Over the days that followed a deep conviction of his sin overwhelmed and on one occasion, whilst taking his lunch break in a nearby forest, such conviction caused him to fall to his knees. Just then, a Scripture verse dropped into his mind:

> *'Then shall you find Me when you search for*
> *Me with all of your heart.' (Jer. 29:13)*

Such a revelation caused his faith to move from the head to the heart. He returned to his law offices and began to play and sing hymns which caused him to weep. Later that day, finding himself alone in one of the offices, he began to pray and then it happened:

> *'There was no fire, no light in the room, nevertheless*
> *it appeared to me as perfectly light…. It seemed as if I*
> *met the Lord Jesus Christ face to face. It seemed to me*
> *a reality that He stood before me and I fell down at*
> *His feet and poured out my soul to Him. I wept aloud*
> *like a child and bathed His feet with my tears.'[74]*

After a long while in this state, Finney returned to another part of the building. As he took a seat next to the fire-place he experienced what he called 'a mighty baptism of the Holy Ghost'. The Spirit descended on him and through his body and soul like a wave of electricity. It seemed like 'the very breath of God' which fanned him 'like immense wings.'[75]

In his autobiography, Finney goes on to describe a feeling of great 'joy' and how he 'bellowed out unutterable gushings from his heart' in waves 'over and over again.' Later that evening, a church choir member, knocking on his door, found him loudly weeping and asked if he was sick or in pain!

The following morning, and throughout the next day, every encounter with the lost led to powerful conviction and conversion. The first man he spoke to was his boss, Judge Wright, who was struck with such conviction that he could not look at the young lawyer. He found Christ a few days later in the same forest where Finney had encountered God some days previously. The second visitor that day was a client who wanted the newly converted barrister to try a case for him. Finney replied with the words:

*'I have a retainer from the Lord Jesus to plead
His cause and I cannot plead yours.'[76]*

The next person that Finney encountered that day was a Universalist[77] in a local shop. His argument was demolished and he soon headed over the fence to the nearby wood to 'get right with God.'

It was clear that from the day of his conversion and Spirit-baptism, Finney was destined to leave the law profession and enter the ministry and 'a life of fire and power such as there have been few parallels in Christian history.'[78] This can be seen from the following examples:

*'Finney was invited to speak in a factory and became
the butt of somewhat ribald humour. Bat as he looked
at the girls who were ridiculing him, a deep solemnity
fell over the room. The owner ordered production to
stop so that Finney could preach the gospel. Most of the
girls were converted. There was a similar occurrence
when Finney was faced with a noisey and drunken
congregation of men who had come to make trouble.*

*As he expounded the story of Lot's wife, the ribaldry
stopped. Soon cries for mercy replaced the coarse
comments that had at first greeted the preacher.'[79]*

Like all men and women of God, Finney had his faults – which
he was always quick to acknowledge and was willing to change.
However, his ministry was marked by an emphasis on the power
of the Holy Spirit and the simplicity of trust in Christ as the key to
all victory. It is estimated that over 80% of his converts remained
true to Christ. He maintained a lawyer's mind in his presentation
of truth, was a man of prayer, believed strongly in both the free
will of man and the sovereignty of God and stressed the importance of personal holiness. He was radical for his time by allowing
women to pray, 'naming and shaming' those in his meetings who
he felt were resisting God and his meetings usually went on for
several hours, often with an element of chaos. On one occasion, a
man came to one of Finney's revival meetings with a pistol, intent
on killing the preacher. Instead he fell to the floor and was saved
by the end of the evening.

Despite opposition, there was no denying, even by his critics, that
God was using him at 'such a time as this' in American history
to shake not only individuals, but cities and the nation itself. It
would be safe to say that his life and writings influenced more
people towards revival and social reform than any other preacher
of the 19th century. He was born before the American Civil War
and hated slavery with a passion. When he became president of
Oberlin College he did so on the express condition that the school
be thoroughly integrated

Finney's long and fruitful ministry lasted some 40 years and over
this time 'thousands found peace in believing. Fortunately, for the
generations that followed, Finney had committed to print many
of his evangelistic ideas and his principles of true revival.'[80] He
outlived three wives and passed away peacefully in Oberlin, Ohio
on the 16th August, 1875 at the age of 82. Written on his tomb-

stone are his memorable words:

> *'The Lord be with us as He was with our*
> *fathers; let us not fail nor forsake him.'*

Lessons to be learned from the 1st and 2nd 'Great Awakenings'

Whilst the Great Reformation of the 16th century attempted to return the Church to many of the principles of New Testament Christianity, the 'Awakenings' of the 18th and 19th centuries sought to bring her even closer to the teachings and practice of the Early Church era. It sought to do this in three main areas:

1. Responsibility of man

The theological tension regarding how much of salvation is attributed to divine ruler ship and how much is man's response, has been hotly debated for centuries. It was Augustine of Hippo in the late 4th century who laid the emphasis on salvation being, in essence, 'everything of God', mainly in response to his adversary, Pelgius,[81] who stressed the opposite – 'everything is of man'. The debate was reignited over a thousand years later through the teachings of John Calvin and the Dutch theologian, Jacob Arminius and continues to this day.

In brief, the question at the heart of the issue was, and is, this – 'if salvation is of the Lord, does man have the ability to respond freely to God to receive this salvation?' Interestingly, the doctrine of 'free will' seems to have been generally accepted in the Early Church era. Not a single orthodox church figure in the first 300 years rejected it, except recognised heretical groups such as the Marcionites, Valentinians and the Manichees. According to Forster and Marsden, in the first four centuries, to reject free will was heresy, free will is a gift given to man by God and man has free will because he is made in God's image and God has free will.[82] It should be stressed at this stage that this gift of free will was not un-limited – i.e. man was not free to save himself or to earn fa-vour with God. The message of Paul is clear, we are justified by faith (Gal. 2:16), by grace and not by works (Eph. 2:8-9). However, despite such limitations, the Early Church did not teach that 'such grace was 'irresistible' or that human beings were not really free to reject or respond to God's Spirit.'[83]

With reference to the First and Second Awakenings, what-ever side of the 'fence' the revivalists stood – whether they were Calvinist, such as Whitefield, or Arminian, such as Wesley – all believed in man's responsibility in the salvation process. Whitefield, for example, with his view of divine election as selection, believed that those who responded to the gospel were the elect. To Wesley, those who responded to gospel preaching were saved according to divine knowledge, not divine planning. Also, of utmost importance, these re-vivalists were convinced that Christ died for all men and that if the 'whosoever' believed, they would gain eternal life (John 3:16). Preaching the gospel was therefore paramount so that all could hear and be given the chance to respond (Rom. 10:14ff). Thankfully, there have always been those such as William Carey (b. 1761). When enquiring about overseas missions he was told in no uncertain terms to:

'Sit down! When God wants to reach the heathen,
He will do it without your help.'

However, the young shoemaker from Northampton made sure he did not 'sit down' and after an extremely fruitful ministry abroad, became known as the Father and Founder of Foreign Missions. It was clear to such men that although God plays a significant role in the salvation of individuals, man has to play his part. How much is of one or the other remains a mystery.

2. Return to the Spirit

Although it would be stretching the point to describe such 'Kingdom greats' as John Wesley and Charles Finney as 'Pentecostals' in the strictest and contemporary sense of the word, there was certainly an emphasis on the work of the Spirit in both their teaching and practice. For example, Wesley records the following experience in his *Journals:*

> '.....with Mr Whitefield and my brother Charles and with
> sixty of our brethren, at about three in the morning,
> as we were continuing in prayer, the power of God
> came mightily upon us. Many cried out and many
> fell to the ground. As soon as we recovered from that
> awe and amazement at the presence of his majesty,
> we broke out in praise with one voice.....'[84]

Although stating his cessationist views at various times of his ministry, on occasions, Wesley did confess to the fact that the Almighty, would manifest his will through extraordinary means including dreams and visions – and that he still does today. This, coupled with the teaching of a second blessing or further endowment of grace to empower the believer to live a life of holiness, did display a pneumatological edge in the teaching and practice of the First Awakening revivalists. Likewise, we have Finney's 'baptism in the Spirit' on the day of his conversion and whether the 'unutterable gushings' experienced on this occasion were tongues or not is unknown. However, it was clear that from the moment of his Spirit-filling, there was incredible power for witnessing (see Acts 1:8) and deep conviction fell on many who came into contact with him. In addition, from a series of lectures given in New York City in 1835, and from the publications these lectures produced, we can be sure of the great emphasis that Finney placed on the role of the Holy Spirit, not only in national revival, but in the life of every believer.

3. Restoration of society
Through the Awakenings of the 18th and 19th centuries came a realisation of the Church's role in being 'salt and light' to a decaying society and both a direct and indirect rediscovery of biblical truth and God's heart for the disadvantaged. For example:

> *'What does the Lord require of you? To act*
> *justly and to love mercy....' (Micah 6:8)*

> *'Religion that God accepts as pure...is this: to look after*
> *orphans and widows in their distress....' (James 1:27)*

> *'...so faith without works is dead.' (James 2:26)*

It is a simple fact that John Wesley's Methodists did more to save England from what could have been the same blood-bath as the French Revolution than any other single factor at the time. The aftermath of the British Awakening saw the influence of Evangelicalism and a renewed interest in the Church for social justice and 'redemption lift'. We have the examples of William Wilberforce (b. 1759) who is chiefly remembered for the abolition of slavery, Elizabeth Fry (b. 1780) and her prison reforms, Lord Shaftesbury's (b. 1801) child labour efforts, not to mention George Muller (b.1805) and Thomas Barnardo (b. 1845) and their orphanage work. In all, there was no 'ostrich in the sand' approach to the world's problems but a realisation of the direct link between conversion and a change in society.

As the First and Second Awakenings, together with later 1857 Revival and the fruitful ministry of D.L. Moody, came to an end, a new awakening for a new century was about to shake the valleys of South Wales and deeply affect its close community – the Welsh Revival.

CHAPTER 8   REVIVAL IN WALES!

'Revive thy work in the midst of the years….' (Hab. 3:2)

As we begin to move into the 20th century and commence a brief study of the Pentecostal Movement, an important precursor to this was the world-renowned Welsh Revival of 1904-1905 which, although not strictly Pentecostal in nature, saw the conversions of several who, themselves, would soon become prominent in British and worldwide Pentecostalism.

The recognised leader of the Welsh Revival was a young man of twenty-six years of age, Evan Roberts. He was a collier boy who became an apprentice in a forge, yet all his young life he had yearned to preach the Gospel. It was said that he was no orator, had received no formal training and was not widely read. In fact, the only book he knew from cover to cover was the Bible, which he carried with him wherever he went. When working in the colliery, he would place it in a convenient nook or hole readily at hand when he could snatch a moment or two to scan its pages. The story is told that a serious explosion occurred underground one day and the future revivalist escaped practically unhurt – although the pages of his Bible were scorched by the fiery blast. The pages that were struck worst by the fire included the account of 2 Chronicles 6-7 where the young Solomon prays for revival!

Indeed, prayer was an important factor to the young Evan, who started praying for some 13 months for a wave of revival to hit the valleys of South Wales. On one occasion he was turned out of his lodgings by his landlady who thought that in his enthusiasm he was possessed or somewhat mad. He spent hours preaching and praying in his room until the lady became afraid of him and asked him to leave.

The young Evan received a divine call to preach and soon started preparation for the Calvinist Methodist ministry. Almost at once, and without question, he was accepted by the people and soon hundreds flocked to his meetings which started at 7.00pm and by 10.00pm had lost none of its passion – with prayer after prayer being offered up, hymns being started spontaneously and with preaching until the early hours of the next morning. Over the course of eighteen months, over 100,000 people were converted and chapels became full once again in the valleys. Notable converts, for the purpose of this study, include D.P. Williams, founder of the Apostolic Church, and George and Stephen Jeffreys. George was the founder of the Elim Pentecostal Church and Stephen saw great success in evangelistic, signs and wonders ministry that resulted in several Assemblies of God churches being planted.

It should be noted that the Welsh Revival had a visible and almost immediate effect on society as, arguably, every true revival should. The local press, both secular and religious, gave the movement much publicity and largely contributed to its rapid spread with the leading dailies 'South Wales News' and the 'Western Mail' devoting three or four columns to it for weeks on end. Stories were told of the local taverns being emptied of its locals who started to attend the revival meetings, old debts were being paid to satisfy consciences, magistrates had very few court cases to preside over, crime plummeted drastically and the miners' pit ponies, used to cursing and swear words, were retired as they no longer understood the commands of their masters.

On reflection, dominant factors of the revival included, prayer, praise and clear preaching on repentance and belief in the crucified Christ – yet in the context of joy and radiant happiness. It is said that Evan Roberts smiled when he prayed, laughed when he sang and preached victory over the dull depression and gloomy doubt of his time. Is it surprising that followers flocked by the thousands to hear him? But what became of Evan Roberts? It was clear from those closest to him that the strain and stress of the numerous meetings began to take its toll and in 1906 he suffered a nervous breakdown. This, coupled with both public and private criticism from other preachers within the Welsh Revival, resulted in Roberts retreating to the home of Jesse Penn-Lewis and her husband where he lived for a number of years as a semi-recluse. He rejected all callers, ignored all letters and even refused to see his own family, choosing instead to write poetry. He co-authored the controversial book *War on the Saints* in which, with Penn-Lewis, he attempts to describe the work of deception in the spiritual world and, in some minds, over-reacting to and doubting even some of the genuine incidents amongst the many pseudo-spiritual events of his own revival. The Welsh Revival, of course, went on – it spread internationally and there were efforts to disciple the converts that had been made. What was God's work, as Roberts had always emphasised, would continue without him. And it did. Evan Roberts only emerged rarely at the end of his life to attend some public religious events, usually unnoticed and to all, but a few, essentially forgotten. He died in 1951 at the age of 73.

At the same time as these miraculous events in the valleys of South Wales, the same Spirit was at work across the Atlantic in the 'City of Angels' – Los Angeles.

CHAPTER 9   THE AZUSA STREET OUTPOURING AND BEYOND

'In the last days, God says, I will pour out my
Spirit on all people....' (Acts 2:17)

It is estimated that at the present time there are approximately 600 million Spirit-filled believers throughout the world. What is even more note-worthy is the fact that it all began in the 'humblest of surroundings and amongst the most ordinary of people.'[85] Charles Fox Parham (1873-1929), hailed by some as the 'father of contemporary Pentecostalism'[86] was a Holiness preacher who formed the Bethel Bible College in Topeka, Kansas in 1900. Typical subjects on the curriculum included Justification by Faith, Second Blessing and the Second Coming, though by the end of the first term, a 'hot topic' was being discussed in class – the Baptism in the Holy Spirit. One morning Parham asked his students to spend some time examining the Scriptures for themselves, in particular the Book of Acts, and to answer the question – what is the biblical evidence of Spirit-baptism? In the days that followed, the class returned with their answers and were unanimous in their findings, namely that speaking in tongues was the reoccurring phenomenon and evidence and when student, Agnes Ozman, received the Spirit and spoke in a language she had never learnt on the 1st January 1901, all doubt was removed and others in the School soon followed suit. Within five years, Parham moved his Bible School to larger premises in Houston, Texas when a most significant student, William J. Seymour, started the ten-week course.

Seymour (1870-1922) was a partially sighted, black evangelist from a mixed denominational background and in keeping within strict segregation laws in the Deep South at the time, was required to listen to lectures from the corridor outside the classroom. After his studies were complete Seymour was asked to pastor a Holiness church in Los Angeles, California though this was short-lived as his teaching on the Spirit was seen as contrary to accepted Holiness views at the time and he arrived at church one day to find it had been padlocked to keep him out! With no place to stay, Seymour was invited to the home of Richard Asbury at 214 North Bonnie Brae Street where he soon began to preach in the living room of the home. With great interest in his teaching on Spirit-baptism and increasing numbers gathering, new premises were required. Eventually a semi-derelict building at 312 Azusa Street, previously used as a livery stable, was chosen and in April 1906 meetings commenced. Within days, scores of people began to fall under the power of the Spirit and arose speaking in tongues.[87] The Azusa Street Mission began to grow at an unparalleled speed with the building soon packed to capacity and with tongues, prophecy, singing in the Spirit and fervent prayer becoming regular features of the services, which continued each night as long as anyone was left in the building! Soon, news spread far and wide through newspaper reports and word of mouth and both the skeptic and the seeker arrived in droves to observe first-hand the events in downtown Los Angeles.

Pentecost in Europe

One such 'seeker' was a Norwegian Methodist minister Thomas Ball Barratt (1862-1940). Barratt was born in Cornwall but at the age of five his parents had emigrated to Norway where later he took further studies in Art and Music, under the supervision of Edvard Grieg. In 1906, as an employee of the Christiana (Oslo) City Mission, Barratt was asked by his church to raise much needed funds for their ministry, though after a year of itinerating in the USA, there was little fruit to show for his labours. Whilst in New York City, planning his return to Oslo, Barratt read an article of the phenomenal events at Azusa Street. Due to the fact that he was running short of funds, he decided not to make the 3000-mile journey to Los Angeles but instead wrote to the Azusa Street Mission to find out more. Within a few weeks, Barratt received a response which convinced him that the happenings at the Mission was 'as at the beginning', as recorded in the Book of Acts and which encouraged Barratt to 'pray and believe for tongues'. On the 7th October 1906, before returning to Europe, Barratt did, indeed, 'pray and believe' and was baptised in the Holy Spirit at the hands of a Sister Maud Williams. He later spoke in tongues on the 15th November 1906.

On his return to Norway, Barratt reported his failed fund-raising efforts to his superiors and much to their displeasure began holding Pentecostal meetings all over the country similar to those at Azusa Street. Within a year or so, the Pentecostal Movement was established in Scandinavia and Barratt went on to open the influential Filadelfia Church in central Oslo and became the President of the European Pentecostal conference in Stockholm in 1939.

Stirrings in Sunderland

Alexander Boddy (1854-1930) was the Evangelical Anglican Vicar at All Saints', Monkwearmouth in Sunderland at the beginning of the 20th century. As a visitor to the Welsh Revival in 1904 he was deeply impressed with what he saw under the ministry of Evan Roberts where some 100,000 people, during an eighteen-month period, came under the conviction of sin and were converted to Christ. On his return to his parish in Sunderland Boddy, together with his wife, Mary, began to seek for a similar revival to affect the North East of England. Evan Roberts, himself, was invited to conduct meetings at All Saints' though he declined the offer. This was, in all probability, providential as reports of Azusa Street were brought to Boddy's attention. As a seasoned traveler and Fellow of the Royal Geographical Society, the vicar made plans to visit Los Angeles, some 6000 miles away to witness, first hand, the Spirit's outpouring. However, before his travel plans were finalised, Boddy heard reports of T.B. Barratt's ministry and similar happenings in Norway and deciding to save himself the longer and more expensive journey to the USA, he made plans to travel to Scandinavia instead. After arriving and witnessing the scenes under Barratt, Boddy recorded in his diary:

> 'My four days in Oslo can never be forgotten. I had stood with Evan Roberts in Tonypandy, but have never witnessed such scenes as those in Norway.'[88]

In Oslo, Boddy experienced impassioned preaching of the gospel but also there was opportunity for the laying on of hands for the receiving of the Spirit with the gift of tongues. He took the opportunity to invite Barratt to visit Sunderland at the end of the summer of 1907 and in preparation for this visit, Boddy wrote and distributed thousands of copies of a pamphlet entitled *Pentecost for England* at the popular Keswick Convention that year. In his opening sentences Boddy claimed:

> 'It is said that 20,000 people today are speaking in tongues around the world, or have so spoken...yet not more than perhaps half a dozen persons are known by the writer to have had this experience in Britain.'[89]

Barratt arrived in Newcastle in early September 1907 and on the evening of his arrival, the first prayer meeting was held in the vestry of All Saints', where they experienced 'great blessings'. Services and prayer meetings followed in the large Parish Hall every afternoon and evening, with a 'waiting meeting' in the vestry after each service that usually continued far into the next morning! Despite opposition from other influential Christian personalities, the meetings grew steadily both in numbers and influence with some national and local daily newspapers recording the events. Although such secular reports were often tinged with cynicism, they proved beneficial by informing large numbers of Christian in Britain of the happenings in the North East. The religious periodicals as a whole, however, maintained a somewhat 'frigid silence' on Barratt's visit, which came to an end on the 18th October 1907 after seven weeks of continual ministry.

After Barratt's return to Norway, a constant stream of seekers continued to visit All Saints' to see and hear for themselves the scenes of the reported Pentecostal phenomena. Many received a personal, tongues-attested Spirit-baptism during this time. It was vital during this early years to both defend and develop the fledgling Pentecostal Movement in Britain and in order to do this, Boddy started an annual Whitsuntide Convention in Sunderland in 1908 and over the years than ensued those that attended included the future pioneers of the larger Pentecostal denominations in Britain, namely George Jeffreys (founder of Elim), Howard and John Carter (founders of Assemblies of God) and D.P. Williams (founder of the Apostolic Church). In addition to the annual conference, Boddy started Britain's first Pentecostal magazine, *Confidence*, which eventually ran from 1908-1926 and at its height, had a weekly readership of 7000. This magazine greatly helped to both propagate Pentecostal doctrine and protect the new movement in its early years of opposition and misunderstanding. It should also be noted that Boddy and his colleague, fellow Anglican, Cecil Polhill, started the Pentecostal Missionary Union (PMU) in January 1909 – described as Britain's, if not the world's, first Pentecostal missionary agency.[90] The PMU started a Men's Training Home in June 1909 and a Women's Training Home in 1910 where Pentecostal missionaries were trained and then sent to various continents of the world.

New Fellowships

It would be safe to say that the purpose of Boddy's and Polhill's efforts through the PMU, the Whitsuntide Convention and *Confidence* was not to create new denominations but to revive the mainstream denominations in Britain – however, this was to come later in the century through the so-called Charismatic Movement. Those who attended the annual Whitsuntide Convention were exhorted to return to their local churches to preach the full and foursquare gospel – Jesus as Saviour, Healer, Spirit-Baptiser and Soon Coming King! However, although such encouragement sounded good in theory, it was a different story in practice. Many of these believers were put out of their churches for their new found Pentecostal beliefs and were generally viewed as fanatics, heretics or even demon-possessed! Some of the bitterest enemies of the Pentecostals were fervent Evangelicals: Baptists, Methodists and Brethren and Christian 'heavy-weights' such as Campbell Morgan, Jesse Penn-Lewis, Reader Harris and F.B. Meyer all joined the attack. With the threat and reality of World War 1, it was becoming clear that it was not possible to pour 'new wine into old wineskins' and when given the choice, to 'keep quiet or leave the church' many early Pentecostals knew the time had come to 'do a new thing' and create new fellowships of churches to gather like-minded believers who had been rejected by their denominations. In 1915, D.P. Williams began the Apostolic Church in South Wales, George Jeffreys started the Elim Evangelistic Band in the same year and in February 1924, in an upper room over a garage in Aston, Birmingham, the Assemblies of God was formed with 26 assemblies, increasing to 74 assemblies in May 1924. According to its website, AoG (GB) today numbers over 500 churches.[91]

It would be safe to say that a happy and harmonious relationship between the main British Pentecostal denominations have continued to this present day and although each have managed to maintain their distinctiveness, a healthy respect and recognition of our 'partners in the other boats' (Luke 5:7) has prevailed.

CHAPTER 10   CONCLUSION

'I will build my Church….' (Matt. 16:18)

I will conclude how I commenced Chapter 1 - In my view, one of the greatest miracles of the Early Church era is how the Church of Jesus Christ was started, grew, spread and triumphed against all the odds and despite tremendous pressure. If the 'Gamaliel test' is to be believed, the fact that 2000 years later the Church is still 'alive and kicking', thriving and not just surviving - then this community of called-out people is not of human origin, but of God (Acts 5:38-39). This reality had already been confirmed by Jesus, Himself in Matt. 16:18 – 'I will build my Church and the gates of hell will not overcome it.' This statement gives four important reassurances:

Firstly, we see the **promise** of Jesus – He *will* build his Church both local and total and when the Lord makes a promise, He always keeps it. He said *'I will send my Spirit'* and He has. He said *'I will come again'* and He will. He said *'I will build my Church'* and He is.

Secondly, we see that it's a **personal** work – It's Jesus' work! He will build *His* Church and unless He does so, regardless of our good intentions, we labour in vain. He is at one with, and personally involved in, His Church to such an extent that to persecute God's people is to persecute God Himself (see Acts 9:1-5). The Church is a building, the Church is a body, but it is also Christ's bride and the Bridegroom is coming for one who is spotless, pure and ready!

Thirdly, He is building his *Church*. Contrary to popular belief, the Church is not a building made out of dead bricks, but living stones. Fallible people made up from every area of life, every nation, tribe and language.

Fourthly, we see the Lord's **protection** – the gates of hell will not prevail. As can be seen through this short work, the Church of Jesus has experienced hardship, crises and more than its fair share of opposition throughout its 2000 year history – yet it remains stronger than ever.[92]

The aim of this booklet has been to give some brief highlights from the Church's long history. It is my view that any Christian reading and seeking to interpret history must have a providential approach – to bear in mind that contrary to Deism, God has been, and continues to be, ultimately in control of His work. History is His-story! It's about what God has done. However, this same God uses imperfect human channels in achieving His goal and how much is of one or the other, is highly debatable. The Divine Builder has carefully placed His 'bricks' and removed His 'stones' at the right time in accordance with His will and in conjunction with His blueprint.

History cannot be re-enacted, re-created or copied exactly to produce similar results in the present. What has happened has happened and the key is to work with the Heavenly Architect who is always doing a new thing (Isaiah 43:19). However, although history cannot be lived in, it can be learned from. I trust that in some way this small offering has taught some lessons from the past to help us in the future.

Steven Jenkins has been in full-time Christian ministry for over twenty-five years and was on the faculty of Mattersey Hall Bible College in the UK for eighteen years, latterly serving as Vice Principal and Lecturer in Early Church History and Church History Survey. He currently exercises an itinerant ministry both at home and abroad and serves on the Board of several Christian organisations in the UK. His theological qualifications include a Diploma in Religious Studies from Cambridge University, an MA in Pentecostal & Charismatic Studies from the University of Sheffield and a professional doctorate in Pentecostal History & Education from the University of Chester.

[1] The word 'history' is derived from the Greek word '*historeo*' and a form of this word is found in Galatians 1:18, translated as 'acquainted with' (*historiasia*).

[2] Tony Lane, *The Lion Concise Book of Christian Thought* (Herts: Lion, 1984), p. 7

[3] Foxe's Book of Martyrs (PA: Whitaker House, 1981) documents the deaths of the Eleven. Interestingly, the word 'witness' is '*martyreo*' - where we get the word 'martyr'.

[4] W.H.C. Frend, *The Early Church* (London: SCM, 1982), p. 6

[5] Eusebius of Caesarea, *History of the Church* II, 3, 1-2; III, 1, 1-3

[6] J. Comby, *How to Understand the History of Christian Mission* (London: SCM, 1996), p. 7

[7] *Against Celsus*, III, 9

[8] Apology 50

[9] H. Bettenson, *The Early Christian Father* (Oxford: OUP, 1986), p. 141

[10] Bettenson, *The Early Christian Fathers*, p. 45

[11] For example, Justin Martyr states: '*We are called atheists and we are as far as the gods of this sort are concerned*' (1 Apology 46).

[12] J.W.C. Wand, *A History of the Early Church* (London: Methuen, 1982), p. 18

[13] The word 'apologist' and 'apologetics' is derived from the Greek word '*apologia*' and can literally mean 'a word that is sent forth' or simply 'a defence'. A form of this word is used in Acts 26:2 – 'in defence

of....'

[14] The word 'creed' comes from the Latin word, *Credo*, meaning 'I believe'

[15] Though 'white' magic and the public consulting of mediums were allowed.

[16] D. Allen, *There is a River* (Milton Keynes: Authentic, 2004), p. 21

[17] The word is derived from the Greek *monos*, meaning 'alone'.

[18] Pope, from the Latin *'pappa'* or Greek *'pappas'*

[19] Montanism was founded in the mid to late 2nd century in Asia Minor. The Montanists had a high view of spiritual gifts, especially the practice of prophecy, though the way their prophecies were communicated, the words that they used and the authority they placed on prophecy brought them condemnation by the wider church.

[20] *Against Heresies* 3:3:2

[21] Allen, *There is a River*, p. 31

[22] Renwick & Harman, *The Story of the Church* (Leicester: IVP, 1958), p. 77

[23] Renwick & Harman, *The Story of the Church*, p. 77

[24] His name most probably came from the root of *beodan*, which means 'to bid or to command'.

[25] Paolo O. Pirlo, *St Venerable Bede* (Quality Catholic Publications, 1997), p. 104

[26] Such wars were known as the Crusades, where great effort was made in order to remove the Saracens from their occupation of the Holy Land with its 'holy places'.

[27] Lane, *Christian Thought*, p. 91

[28] Allen, *There is a River,* p. 42

[29] Allen, *There is a River*, p. 42

[30] Charismatic, in this context, is derived from the Greek word *charismata* which can be interpreted as 'a divinely conferred gift or gifts'.

[31] This was called 'Conciliarism'.

[32] Allen, *There is a River*, 52

[33] C. Geikie, *The English Reformation* (Strahan & Co, 1879), p. 114

[34] C. Beard, *Martin Luther and the Reformation* (Paternoster, 1889), p. 156

[35] Beard, *Martin Luther*, p. 165

[36] W. Pratney, *Revival* (Whitaker House, 1983), p. 37

[37] Pratney, *Revival*, p. 39

[38] The doctrine of Purgatory had been devised and developed to take into account the many people who were not ready for heaven at the time of death. Purgatory was an in-between state for the purpose of purification or purgation.

[39] This is discussed in Luther's *To the Christian Nobility of the German Nation* 1520

[40] Beard, *Martin Luther*, p. 432

[41] W. Durant, *The Reformation* (Simon & Schuster, 1957), p. 361

[42] Anabaptists in this context were Reformation-era Christians who rejected infant baptism in favour of believer's baptism.

[43] A Dallimore, *George Whitefield* (Edinburgh: Banner of Truth, 1970), pp. 19-27

[44] Deism, amongst other things, denied the activity of a Creator with his creation.

[45] It could be argued, therefore, that Charles was the true founder of 'Methodism'.

[46] The Moravians were founded by Count von Zinzendorf who established a community called *Herrnhut* (The Lord's Watch) in 1724. Shortly after, a prayer meeting was started which lasted some 100 years.

[47] J. Wesley, *Journals* (Connecticut: Keats, 1979), p. 8

[48] Wesley, *Journals*, p. 29

[49] Page 43

[50] J. C. Ryle, *Christian Leaders of the 18th Century* (Edinburgh: Banner of Truth, 1978), p. 78

[51] Allen, *There is a River*, pp. 81-82

[52] H. Snyder, *The Radical Wesley* (Leicester: IVP, 1980)

[53] A 'cessationist' would generally believe that the gifts of the Spirit mentioned in such passages as 1 Corinthians 12, ended or ceased with the Early Church or with the apostles in the First Century AD.

[54] Donald Dayton, for example, traces the beginnings of 20th century and current day Pentecostalism to Methodism in his book: *Theological Roots of Pentecostalism* (Michigan: Hendrickson, 1987)

[55] Ryle, *Christian Leaders of the 18th Century*, p. 31

[56] Whitefield, *Journals*, p. 52

[57] Asceticism is from the Greek meaning 'training' and can be de-

scribed as the abstinence of certain worldly pleasures in the pursuit of spiritual goals.

[58] Dallimore, *George Whitefield*, p. 77

[59] Ryle, *Christian Leaders*, p. 49

[60] A podium and plaque marking this spot is still in existence today

[61] Pratney, *Revival*, p. 111

[62] H. Fischer, *Reviving Revivals* (Gospel Publishing House, 1950), pp. 165-166

[63] L. Drummond, *The Awakening That Must Come* (Boardman, 1978) p.15

[64] Drummond, *The Awakening*, pp. 15-16

[65] M. Taylor, *Exploring Evangelism* (Beacon Hill, 1964), p.142

[66] Pratney, *Revival*, p. 115

[67] A circuit rider was a Methodist ministerial role originated by John Wesley. Each circuit of congregations sometimes numbered as many as 25 or 30 meeting places which was under the supervision of a senior Methodist preacher who often had several lay assistants. Any young man who could preach and was willing to ride a horse for weeks on end over wild country might become an assistant and finally a circuit rider. Circuit riders numbered about 100 by the end of the Revolutionary War in 1783. The salary was $64 a year until 1800 when it was raised to $100. There were few actual meetinghouses – church services were usually held in cabins, in barrooms or outdoors. (www.britannica.com/topic/circuit-rider)

[68]   www.christianity.com/church/church-history/timeline/1701-1800/peter-cartwright-colorful-preacher

[69] On one occasion, Cartwright warned General Andrew Jackson (future President of the US from 1829-1837) that he would be damned to Hell just as quickly as any other man if he did not repent!

[70] A circuit rider was a Methodist ministerial role originated by John Wesley. Each circuit of congregations sometimes numbered as many as 25 or 30 meeting places which was under the supervision of a senior Methodist preacher who often had several lay assistants. Any young man who could preach and was willing to ride a horse for weeks on end over wild country might become an assistant and finally a circuit rider. Circuit riders numbered about 100 by the end of the Revolutionary War in 1783. The salary was $64 a year until 1800 when it was raised to $100. There were few actual meetinghouses – church services were usually held in cabins, in barrooms or outdoors. (www.britannica.com/topic/circuit-rider)

[71]   www.christianity.com/church/church-history/timeline/1701-1800/peter-cartwright-colorful-preacher

[72] On one occasion, Cartwright warned General Andrew Jackson (future President of the US from 1829-1837) that he would be damned to Hell just as

quickly as any other man if he did not repent!

[73] Charles Finney, *Autobiography* (Bethany, 1979), p. 12

[74] Finney, *Autobiography*, p. 21

[75] Finney, *Autobiography*, p. 22

[76] Finney, *Autobiography*, p. 26

[77] A belief that all people will ultimately be saved – some would argue that this happens through Jesus' atoning death, others without Christ.

[78] Pratney, *Revival*, p. 122

[79] Allen, *There is a River*, p. 111

[80] C. Finney, *Lectures on Revival* (Bethany, 1976), cover page

[81] Pelagius believed that man was not born a sinner and therefore has perfect freedom to do either right or wrong.

[82] R. Forster & P. Marsden, *God's Strategy in Human History* (Tyndale, 1973), p. 244

[83] Pratney, *Revival*, p. 130

[84] *Journals of John Wesley*, Vol. II, p. 125

[85] Allen, *There is a River*, p. 122

[86] K. Kendrick, *The Promise Fulfilled* (Springfield, MO: Gospel Publishing House, 1961), p. 36

[87] V. Synan, *The Holiness Pentecostal Movement in the U.S.* (USA: Eerdmans, 1971), p. 107

[88] W. Kay, *Pentecostals in Britain* (Paternoster, 2000), p. 12

[89] D. Gee, *Wind and Flame* (Heath Press Ltd, 1967), pp. 20-21

[90] Burgess & McGee, *Dictionary of Pentecostal & Charismatic Movements* (Michigan: Zondervan, 1988), p. 706

[91] www.aog.org.uk

[92] According to Barrett's 'World Christian Encyclopaedia' some 2.7 million people are converted to Christianity every year (2001, p. 360)

Printed in Great Britain
by Amazon